The collective dreamer

harpreet lakhan

ISBN: 978-1-7777217-0-1

A sad girl's diary

A collection of poems
that I have written while processing grief
so that I can create more room in my heart for love

Perhaps my dreams will help me understand
why I take all these drugs to expand
my mind, my heart and my freedom
maybe that will help me understand where I come from

I am all my past lives combined into one

- *Moksha*

When I look at you
I see myself
everything that I have owned
everything that I have disowned
the things I love
the things I would like to change
but most importantly
I see the love
I radiate

- Mirrors

If I could live anywhere
it would be by the mountains
through the alleyway
into the fountains
of water, of streams and everything else in between
I'd sit by the window and have a cup of coffee
I'd indulge in luxury
and see what it takes to stop me
I'd hike every mountain
until there is nothing more to see
I'd get to the top and know this is exactly
where I'm meant to be

- Mountains

Your darkest parts
aren't even that dark
but you have to realize that

- *Mother ayahuasca*

I am a healer
a giver
I stand tall and fight through every obstacle
with my masculine energy
and yet
still remain soft and graceful
leaving my feminine touch
everywhere I go and in every heart I touch

- The masculine and feminine

The collective dreamer

I have gone on a journey
across the oceans
and beyond the seas
only to come back
to who I always been

- I was never lost

I am no longer grieving
but that doesn't mean I am not hurting
it just means the hardest part is done

Before he hit me
he made sure I had eaten
and was clothed
what I think I'm trying to say is
I think he cares
what I mean by that is
he isn't all bad
but I question
how can the hands that feed me
be the same hands that leave me feeling
unworthy

- My father's hands

The hardest thing to accept has been
no matter how strong a woman may be
the power a man holds
will always be greater

- I'm sorry it had to be this way

The collective dreamer

Now that I have picked up my family's pieces
I can focus on myself and see what releases

I feel so much guilt
knowing that
healing is a privilege
many can't afford

- *First generation*

I am tired of routine
I am tired of inconsistency
I think I am just tired of feeling so deeply
I am tired of my mind
I am not sure what it is I am trying to find

I can't seem to tell
if my imagination is
a form of escapism

- *Whose side you are on*

.

I hope you understand
this was not part of the plan
but you should have known
that I loved myself
more than I loved you
that shouldn't have come as a surprise
you saw it in my lack of compromise
there is nothing wrong with you
but I just need a change of view

- Faithful to myself

If you see me dancing with myself
please don't think you can join
you are not my equal
collect your bags
and get the fuck out of my sequel

- I Dance

How much confusions it brings
when you can't tell the difference
between butterflies and your own intuition

- Instinct

When I close my eyes
I can see
everything I dreamt of being
when I open my eyes
I realize
I have already become that person

- Manifestation

The collective dreamer

I have spent lifetimes
looking for the right answers
only to realize
they have been looking for me too

How amazing it is to feel
when a path isn't right for me
when a person isn't right for me
all over my body I feel a sensation
in the pit of my stomach
I feel the rejection

The leaves may change
but the roots remain
and just as so
I will never sway
too far away

- Grounded

I hope when I rejected you
It turned you to your heart
I hope you were able to learn the lesson
and let in
the rejection
I hope it got you reflecting

- To all the men

I have learned to enjoy things
while they last
there is something permanent
about impermanence

- The non-committed committer

Imagine if break ups and endings were celebrated
because we left eachother
in a better version than we found eachother

- The world I want to live in

The collective dreamer

I am on a journey
that you are not a part of
don't try to catch up

Maybe one day if the stars align
I'll open my heart and share something truly divine

I told you I was like a tree
you thought that meant
I would stay in one place
but I was referring to the leaves that forever
change

- Free spirited

harpreet lakhan

Desired but unattainable

I have decided that I am rich
I am rich in experiences
I am rich in love
the foods that I eat are rich in flavour and healthy
ingredients
I am rich in health
I am rich in knowledge
I'm filled with wisdom money can't buy
I am rich from the laughter I share with my loved ones
I have everything that I need
and nothing that I don't
my mind is rich
with creativity, thoughts and ideas
I am debt free because I have given my all
in every past and present relationship
I am rich because I wake up every morning and go to
bed every night with peace on my mind
I am filled with so many riches that others simply cannot
see

- Money mantra

The sun would be envious
if it could see
the light inside of me

- Solar plexus

I am done hiding
how much I love myself
why don't you observe
to learn
rather than observe
to envy

harpreet lakhan

I stepped back
so you could stand a chance

- *And you still lost*

As sweet as can be
even the bumble bees
are envious of me

harpreet lakhan

She [women] is not your enemy
she is your ally

And when the world ends
I can only hope
you would choose me again

- In every lifetime

I am realizing which relationships in my life are divine and heart centred. I allow all my relationships to be as they are but I will acknowledge when it is time to let go, re-evaluate and re-arrange.

I can't believe
I have become
the women of my dreams
but then again
I can

You don't need a reason to be loved
you are worthy
simply without reason
existing
is enough

I held my hand and walked myself down the aisle
I am marrying the parts of myself
I never thought were worthy of love

- When in peru

You will go from lady to woman
when your compassion becomes unconditional

- Initiation into womanhood

As delicate as a butterfly's wings
my heart can only be handled
by the most delicate of hands

Thank you for calling me a witch
I know that means I am a woman
that is feared for being true to who I am
and helping those in need when my etheric magic
and that I have done my job to challenge outdated beliefs
to fight for freedom for the vulnerable
when I am vulnerable myself
thank you for calling me a witch
I wear that title with honor
knowing my ancestors before me are giving me the
strength to move forward
generations of women before me have perfected a craft
that has yet to understood by you
thank you for calling me a witch
after lifetimes of being killed
I have reincarnated again to share my magic with the
world

We don't need to speak
for me to understand your language

- Telepathy

It's so easy to suppress your emotions and move on
you convince yourself that you don't care
but then you walk in
and it's like a tsunami of emotions

We lock eyes
pretend we don't care
but do everything we can to be in each other's stare
is this all in my head? is this another illusion?
do you feel the same way or am I just losing – my mind

- Tsunami

And when we were taught
God is outside of us
we began to lose our power

- The hidden agenda

harpreet lakhan

Why does suffering and learning lessons
go hand in hand
can I make an agreement with God
to go easier on me?

Through the union of the divine masculine and divine feminine we go from duality to oneness and the highest potential of the God within is reached

A new earth
will one day exist
and in it
there will be nothing but bliss
we will live from our hearts
and have integrated our shadows
there will be no wars
or never-ending battles

- A new earth

How blessed I am
to be led
from a power that lives within

- Inner compass

harpreet lakhan

I can't help but question of all the fates
why I was given the one with the most amount of grace

God, if this is my last lifetime on earth
please allow me one last time to give birth
to ideas, to beliefs and to anything else
that will allow me to process this grief

God, if this is my last time I experience love
please check mark for me "all of the above"
I want adventure, I want trust
I want everything but empty lust

- A letter to God

God gave her powers no one understood
God gave her powers but no one believed her to be good

- Old Crone

The collective dreamer

Take me away to higher learning
I want to hear words that get my soul burning

No matter how hard it's been
I have never regretted doing the right thing

I promise
to never get too comfortable
and forget where I come from

The rise of colour
has washed out
those living in white

- Minority is the majority

I am humbled by this experience we call life
what a blessing it is
to experience our loved ones
in physical form
before we part ways again

What do I do now
how do I make peace
knowing that my lineage
ends with me

Thank you to all my friends
to the women that have held space
for the depths of my shadows
without judgement
sat with me while I cried
and shared their pain, so I knew I wasn't alone
for the men
who taught me to be comfortable with myself
and showed me how I deserve to be treated
for showing me unconditional acceptance
and making me laugh
I hope my presence has done the same
and has taken away some of your pain

- To friends that turn into family

I'm here
   sitting   and thinking
waiting
     for my turn
eager
  but   not quite there
        yet
     hoping
 wishing   and then
deciding
to   get up
and give
       myself

                         a turn

The collective dreamer

Instead of coming back for more
take what I have given you
and spread it across the world

harpreet lakhan

There is no truth in illusion
and there in no illusion in truth

You have reached the end of what has been a chapter in my life. My intention is to give you glimpse of what my spiritual journey has looked like while processing heartache, relationships in their many forms and finding my place in the world. It seems to me that the answer to all our sorrows is learning self-love, and I don't mean just saying "I love myself" but genuinely feeling what loving yourself feels like in every ounce of your body. I hope you are able to resonate with my words and explore what my short poems mean to you.

Manufactured by Amazon.ca
Bolton, ON

21331673R00039